"Esteem"

Yourself !

by Bob Locker

Dear Kids and Grandkids,

Judy and I grew up in a different world. Getting our "sea legs" in rural Iowa had its advantages. Just let Mom know, and you could go downtown, or fishing at the Little Rock River...and stay all day. There were very few rules, just "be responsible...and come home for supper."

Yes, we even had BB guns.

Now the various governments, from our towns and cities all the way to the nation's capital, want to protect everyone, from everything, all of the time. It should be obvious…that's impossible, expensive, and just plain wrong.

Our personal freedom, and the knowledge and ability to deal with what life throws our way, has all but disappeared, along with our self-esteem.

My baseball career took me away a good part of the time, during your formative years. My grandparenting skills have not been the best either, and I haven't been that available for you, grandchildren.

So, I've spent some time working on something I could give to you.

Here are a few simple guidelines, to help you navigate through life. This little book will fit in your pocket, purse, glove compartment, toolbox ...or whatever, and I put a few blank pages in the back for your own thoughts and ideas about what each day presents. These few pages may not seem like much...but there are no wasted sentences.

It has all you'll need to change your life...and create positive thoughts and deeds.
And success.

Good luck.
Bob

I believe it was 1967, my third year with the White Sox. We were one run ahead in the top of the ninth inning. The bases were loaded, with two out…and one of the game's best left-handed hitters, Eddie Mathews, was at the plate.

We battled through a series of pitches until the count was full. The runners would be going with the next pitch, so the game would be tied if I missed the strike zone, and a hit would probably clear the bases.

I retreated behind the mound, where every pitcher's last source of comfort resides, the rosin bag. I gave it a good squeeze and took a deep breath…as I tried to gather myself.

A remarkable calm settled over me. I had a "Jonathan Livingston Seagull" moment, visualizing a fastball right at the belt, on the inside corner. My sinker had lots of movement and it struck me *that was the place to go* with this critical pitch.

He was making contact with all my low sinkers, and this might freeze him.

It is one of those rare moments that is still ingrained in my memory.

Putting all of the negatives out of my mind, I pictured a positive result… and delivered the pitch…right where I wanted.

As I had hoped, Eddie froze.. and then leaned backed just a little, thinking it was inside. The ball broke back over the inside corner, the umpire raised his right hand… and the game was over.

How did I make that happen?

It was a combination of things, but essentially, it was the culmination of the process of building my belief in myself over many years… and a mysterious element, I call the FORCE, which I will define presently.

Years later, at an "old-timers" game, Eddie came up to me shaking his head.

" I still remember that pitch. How in hell were you able to get your sinker in there? I was looking for it down where you usually threw it."

Yes, Eddie, I still remember it, too.

How to feel good about yourself.

First of all, exactly what is Self-Esteem, my "lynch-pin" to Success? Simply put, it's whatever makes you feel good about yourself. The key words and phrases that follow… are all building blocks that will create your self-esteem.

Your "self," however, is not easily fooled. We all have that potent defense mechanism called rationalization. It often allows us to "get by" even when unbiased logic says… there's a real problem.

When you do what follows, you won't have to "rationalize" anything, and you will feel honestly good about who you are.

Self-esteem permeates all the other things that help you be successful.

Keep in mind these are only my guidelines. You should feel free to tweak them. Discard what's uncomfortable and substitute things you do feel good about.

The key is to do what you honestly believe will work for you.

OK, let's get started.

Plan Ahead
Little steps…
…make long journeys
Anticipate
Never give up

Accept responsibility
Heed your instincts
Esteem yourself
Accommodate failure
Do it!

FORCE, faith, etc.

1. Plan Ahead:

The letters of the phrases on the previous page spell out an *acronym*… just another word for a memory key.

Most of us have used this technique when studying for tests. I hope this little memory aid will stick with you, and help you remember what you need to do. Nothing would please me more than for this to give you a big assist… toward an "A" in life.

I have a close friend who was a professional bike racer. He trained hard for the races, but, several times didn't make it to the starting line on time. The alarm was not set, breakfast got in the way, the car wouldn't start, and so on.

It's hard to win if you're not there when the flag goes down.

When you have a task and a deadline, make a list. Check it twice. The old carpenter's adage… "measure twice and cut once" is so true.

If you **think ahead**, and **plan ahead**, good things are bound to happen.

2. Little steps make long journeys:

As a kid, I dreamed (like millions of others) about becoming a major league baseball player.

It began with those Iowa roots I mentioned, and the ingrained idea that I must be responsible for my actions. Rationalizing the dream was not an option.

Early training was looping a "hand me down" baseball glove over the handle bars and, juggling a bat and dirt-colored ball or two, multi-tasking my way down to Sebring's vacant lot for a pick up game with who ever was available.

That repeated exercise eventually produced a reasonably effective high school pitcher, and a chance to play for the George (Iowa) town team.

Pretty typical of a young, green as the Iowa spring prairie kid, I threw every pitch as hard as I could, but usually up in the strike zone.

My "breaking ball" was a flat curve/slider …that intimidated some inexperienced hitters, but not the good ones.

My choice of colleges was my mother's alma mater, Iowa State University.

I reasoned that since she had turned out to be perfect…there might be a chance for me to amount to something.

I was flattered to get a visit from the longtime coach and mentor, Cap Timm. He was intrigued enough to offer me a room in the dorm under the stadium, and tuition and books.

This was not a big baseball program and Cap didn't have the budget for more than a handful of partial scholarships...like mine.

He was a man respected by his peers, and all of his players, and was one of the few coaches and managers I found during my career, that led by example.

When practices finished, and it was time to drag the infield, there was Cap...shepherding his old Chevy coupe (known as the "Blue Goose") around the familiar route in the dirt portion of the infield.

After the dragging operation, he and the players and he were there together, in the middle of the infield, picking up rocks and debris that might cause a bad bounce.

One day during practice, Cap was standing behind the mound…watching me try and impress him with how hard I could throw. I was busy admiring that my fastball was very "live" and broke back to the right.

However, it was normally up or out of the strike zone.

"Bob, we are not going to find out if you can handle good college hitters until you can get it in the strike zone more often, than not. Why don't you try shortening your stride… bend your front knee, and hang on to the ball a little longer."

An amazing thing happened.

Not only did it generally end up in the strike zone…but occasionally had a distinct downward movement (when it wanted to)…rather than to the right.

Those few words of advice were the beginning of my career out pitch, the "smothered sinker", a rare, but temperamental pitch, that had both velocity and downward movement.

Professional scouts were always looking for pitchers with the ability to throw low strikes that broke down … leading to ground balls, more often than not.

Baseball wisdom was that if you can "throw" four ground balls in a row without walking anyone…you'd likely get three outs before a run scored.

All the day to day effort and little strides I had taken… were nothing compared to this one step.

A chance at professional baseball became a reality, in fact there were three teams that made offers.

I was absolutely shocked, since my college record was pretty mediocre.

The "smothered sinker" was a very temperamental pitch, and I continually fought for the proper grip and motion, making sure to get on top of the pitch at the release point.

It was a constant battle, much like perfecting a knuckle ball delivery. I played with some of the best of my era, including Eddie Fisher, Wilber Wood, and the dean of them all…Hoyt Wilhelm.

Even with the help of all three (on the same White Sox roster) I was never able to perfect the pitch to the point of risking even one in a game.

Few others reached that point, either.

During spring training and throughout the season, I felt I had to do a little more than everyone else. With a depth perception problem, I was never going to be a good hitter or fielder at the professional level.

But, I had a live arm, and I could run. Few… other than my teammates knew that, because I rarely hit a fair ball in the game.

So, I made it a point to do more conditioning than the others. Pitchers are notoriously lazy about "drills" and dreaded the "wind sprints" at the end of practice.

Wanting to get more out of practice, I'd deliberately start behind the pack and "catch up" at the end of each sprint. That way, no one was shown up. I did it the first day of minor league spring training, until the last day of my major league career…. some 14 years later.

As a veteran player, it felt good to have my teammates tell rookies in spring training…. " See that guy… he's the oldest player on the team, but I'll bet he can run you into the ground"

The most daunting tasks can be accomplished by taking one step at a time. Sounds hokey, but it works.

Puzzles are solved by putting the first two pieces together. Then another and another. Marathons start with the first mile… and so on.

Don't be overwhelmed by any goal. Just set a short term objective that's within reach. Once accomplished, look for another achievable point along your path.

Before long you'll surprise yourself when you look up…,and see the goal within sight.

3. Anticipate:

Judy and I went to a University of California, Berkeley basketball game a few years ago…and were intrigued by a freshman guard who showed knowledge and reactions beyond his years. He led the charge that turned a 13 point halftime deficit, into a win... going away.

Without his contribution, it would not have happened, yet he was just a freshman, not the guy you would pick to have the confidence to make "all or nothing" decisions. It was not his defense alone, but anticipating the play, often leaving his man unguarded, that led to an intercepted pass.

Doing something defensively can often be more valuable than a great offense play. Stopping theirs, and giving your team a chance to score, is often a double victory.

Keep that in mind as you set your priorities. Eliminating something bad is twice as valuable as doing something good.   But, that requires anticipation. And it means you must act on your instincts quickly…often instantly.

As I have said before, you must be in a positive frame of mind to make most of these things work….so start with self-esteem… and build it until your "self" is convinced that you feel good about who you are.

4. Never give up:

The keys to the steps to success are related, especially this.

One of my bosses was Charlie Finley, owner of a major league baseball team, the Oakland A's, in the 60's and 70's. Thanks to Charlie, I am the proud possessor of two World Series championship rings.

Engraved on those rings is a simple formula: S+S=S " **Sweat** plus **Sacrifice** equals **Success**". Yes, an acronym.

Although I didn't learn "my formula" from Mr. Finley, he gave all of us the chance to achieve our goal… to be part of the best team in baseball. He accumulated a group of talent that could be very successful, if we worked together.

For that particular year, we were the best team in baseball. And, once achieved, nobody can take it away. Talk about a huge dose of self esteem! Thanks again, Charlie.

What was my formula? See **8. Accommodate Failure,** for the answer.

Professional baseball is the perfect example of what "giving up" can do. Excellent hitters "fail" 70% of the time. The very best pitchers…permit a hit every inning (on average).

My goal was to allow fewer than one hit and/or walk per inning. In other words the batters who got hits or walks (for which I was directly responsible) … would be one per inning, or less.

By doing that more often than not, I achieved very respectable lifetime statistics, even though I was not considered a star. ERA (earned run average) is the best measure of your effectiveness, and a lifetime ERA of 2.75 makes me feel pretty good.

Baseball is also a great example of the results of lost confidence, better known as a "slump". Because it is a "start and stop" sport (nothing happens until the pitcher throws the ball), it is a tempting opportunity to doubt yourself, and let negative thoughts creep in and control the situation.

Let's say you are pitching and have allowed a couple of hits, and the cardinal sin… a base on balls. The pitching coach is on the way to the mound with some advice.

Which would you rather hear?

"Don't give him anything good to hit, don't hang a breaking ball, don't get a pitch inside that he can hit out, and above all, don't walk him".

Wow, what a pile of negatives to chew on!

Or this… "We are in good shape. You've had great success with this guy, especially with that awesome sinker. One ground ball and we're out of the inning. The defense is ready to turn the double play. Go get 'em".

More often than not, pitching coaches, parents, bosses, etc. deliver the first example...what not to do. If, like the second coach, they gave you the gift of positive thoughts, your ability to put your best skills "in play" is greatly enhanced.

You are really your own coach. And if you reinforce yourself with positive thoughts and visualization… you will be an entirely different person.

However, none of these positive reinforcements are enough, unless you concentrate and persevere.

My second career (in real estate) was very much like baseball. It's also a team sport… but you "sink or swim" with your own efforts. Nearly every transaction I have been involved in over the past 30 years, has had one or more critical junctions, where it looked like it was going to fall apart.

That's when you kick it up a notch…and ignore the inexcusable comment with which we are all familiar: "It was not meant to be".

I hate that line.

When I heard that from the realtor representing the other offer, I just smiled and knew that my client was going to get the house.

When it came from my client, they promptly got a polite, but firm, lecture. The field of real estate sales is littered with the bodies of those who tried... and didn't succeed.

I am a member of a small but quality group of realtors who meet monthly to discuss the market, and help each other solve problems. It's made up of at least one person from all of the major firms in the area. They are the **survivors**...those who did not quit, learned to live with rejection…and just plain **outworked** the others. I asked them to review a draft of this little book, because I value their opinion.

I think many smiled and nodded, when they read this section.

OK… I am taking a break. We've done **PLAN** and before we move on to **AHEAD,** I'm using the space between the two to fill in a few other important things you will need to face and conquer. So here goes:

Most of this book is about building esteem, and I must emphasize the building part.

There is no switch to turn on or off.

It is like any workout. Whatever your physical abilities or limitations, you must **work at it** and increase your repetitions, and the stretch the boundaries of your achievements

Esteem is a slow, methodical process. There will be times when you feel like you have not made progress and even lost ground. Stay the course, and you will soon find it was only a lull in a steady upward climb.

Your mind operates in much the same way. Take a "course", and stay on it. Through the classes, midterm, the final preparation, and the final itself. That is how high school, college and advanced degrees evolve. Grab as much "PHD" as you want (and can afford), to "pile on" .

We will continue these building blocks in short order…but there is one other fascinating and crucial element mentioned earlier, that can be with you, **only after** your self-esteem is strong enough to allow it to enter.

It can be there in an instant.

It is called different things…heart, faith, courage, guts, bravery, and a bunch of other descriptive words or short phrases.

Read on… and you will have my way to help remember… and let it in.

An outstanding example was Hoyt Wilhelm, one of the most successful baseball pitchers in the history of the game. I mentioned him before. It was my privilege to play with Hoyt for several years, with the White Sox.

In street clothes, you would never suspect he was an athlete, much less a professional baseball player who was destined for the Hall of Fame.

Although many owners, managers, scouts and others don't seem to realize it, baseball is a game of statistics, that judge you on your actual results, not your vertical leap or your 40-yard dash time, especially, if your job is to throw the ball.

He was a small, prematurely balding man, with a few too many inches around the middle and the look of an economics professor. This was compounded by a malady of some sort which forced him to cock his head to the side just to straighten out the world. That earned him his nickname…Tilt.

He threw a fastball that topped out in the mid seventies….and little else.

Except he learned how to throw the knuckle ball...better than anyone in baseball history. Look up his lifetime statistics… and you will be amazed.

The knuckleball is like a butterfly, that doesn't know where it is going. It has a mind of its own, and requires complete concentration and faith.

Exactly what is faith? I will define it as belief, without needing absolute proof. I am not talking about religious faith... faith in God. That is another book, and far beyond tackling here...

No, I am talking about faith in one's **self.** And, Hoyt had it... in spades.

How else could you throw a baseball with the lowest velocity of anyone in the history of professional baseball, cause it to approach the plate with absolutely no spin... and just as it was about to come into range of the hitter, make the raised seams of the ball, react with the air currents, creating abrupt movement in almost any direction (except up).... and still get it in the strike zone!

There I've said it... the longest sentence in this book... and I need a breath.

I have seen him completely frustrate some of the best hitters in the game.

One of the most vivid examples was watching powerful Willie Horton of the Tigers, start his swing at a pitch in his eyes....and complete the comedy by breaking his bat on home plate.

Hoyt held his glove up to his face to hide the grin. Nobody wanted to make Willie mad.

Although professional athletes universally have strong wills, Hoyt was the best example of it properly used, that I have ever seen.

You will recall that I tried to be in better physical shape than my teammates and that included extra stamina. I did it partly because I was afraid I didn't have enough physical skills necessary to succeed at the major league level.

This force is both diverse and omnipotent. It can be called upon for a moment… or again and again, to see you through more lengthy tribulations and challenges.

But, there is a danger here….

Many star athletes, politicians, and, yes, evangelist ministers, had high degrees of "self-worth" at least during their careers. But, they did not have the benefit of a book like this, to help create this "confidence" the right way.

Often, it was made up mainly of ego, power, and yes, success with little regard (and respect) for others, which sometimes led them to think they could do anything they wanted.

Some keep it, and others lose this magic ingredient when they do something to cause their self esteem to crumble. You put your own spins on the list below:

Michael Jordan, Reggie Jackson…Reverend Jesse Jackson (strange similarity here), OJ Simpson,

Lance Armstrong, Bruce Jenner, Terrell Owens, Rick Barry, Bill Clinton, Jerry Falwell, Dennis Rodman, Richard Nixon, Tammy Faye Baker and her buddy "what's his name", Denny McClain, Pete Rose, and Tiger Woods come to mind.

There are lots of people who became well known, and got a little bit too impressed with themselves..

I could give a long list of senators and congressmen, but what's the point? In politics, it seems to be a universal phenomenon.

Common Sense can do more toward solving a problem than just about anything else. To get a grasp on a task, you must see the big picture. It is easy to become buried in the details and never see the light of day. Engineers tend to have "minutia" disease. If you become one…remember to take your daily dose of lessons from this book to prevent that from surfacing.

Common sense is also the glue that bonds everything together. Don't get too smart for your own good.

Try to avoid "pigeonholing" your thinking and your actions. Instead, stand back as faaaaaarrrrr as you can... and see what is really going on.

The way to do that is...to **listen.** It is difficult, because we often "tune out" as soon as we think we know what the other person is going to say. This was one of my most difficult lessons to learn. Not until, perhaps 15 years ago, did I realize how important that was, and how little listening I really did.

While working on real estate remodeling projects…I often hired help but managed the project myself.   After a few years of frustration, I learned a valuable technique.

I'd give the crew a straight-forward one sentence summary of what we were to do. After "do you understand?" and the agreeable nods…I would ask them to repeat what I just said. Try it, and you will understand what happens better than just telling you.

Look at all parts of an issue, including the other side. Put yourself in their shoes. Once you really understand what is "in the way", you've gone a long way toward solving the problem.

Like all the other keys to this booklet, everything is linked to **self-esteem,** the "lightning rod" connecting them all.

Up to now we have been dealing mainly with things which build your physical and mental strength to deal with life on a daily basis.

But, there are also periods… from moments to months, that you will be severely tested. It could be as brief and fleeting as facing as six foot putt to win the golf match, or as critical and prolonged as finding you have a life threatening illness. That's when you will need all your new found self assurance.. which is the key to unlocking the most important and potent ingredient.

You have heard it called heart, spirit guts, bravery, and a number of catchy phrases. It sums up pretty well as **"will power"**.

Many of you will remember the "Star Wars" movies and the various characters who uttered a version of this cult-like phrase.

I specifically recall the character, Darth Vader. He made that line…"May the force be with you"….especially vivid for me.

This is powerful stuff, but hard to define. Let's take a look at **FORCE…** and a way to remember what makes this so potent…

Focus...
On...
Remarkable, but...
Calm...
Execution, during those critical times that come in all of our lives.

You might question why I used the word "remarkable." You're right, I needed an R, but if you look a little further, it has more depth than you might think. I have read a few medical charts and thought it odd that they kept referring to various test results as "unremarkable."

So, having nothing to remark about is very good news.

Conversely, when you can make it "remarkable"...that is, not just good, it is outstanding!

The other word choice that may seem odd, is "calm". It may be the most important link to harnessing this force and all of its elements.

This needs another example:

I was extremely nervous during the baseball game, not the best quality for a late inning relief pitcher.

But, I was able to pull myself together when the phone rang, but it did make the anxiety tough to handle. I finally found a way to slow things down and maintain a reasonably calm state of mind.

After a couple of years with the White Sox, I had reached the point that it was unlikely I would be called into the game before the late innings.

The bullpen was tucked under the stands in center field, so it was pretty invisible to most of the fans. The dark green walls added to its nickname, the "dungeon."

Long naps can leave a person groggy and a little dysfunctional, but short "cat naps" of 15 minutes or less, are both refreshing and calming. I found that "missing" the 5th or 6th inning….left me relaxed, refreshed, and focused when the game tightened in the late innings, and my number got called.

I soon discovered ways to do my little "sessions" on the road and in more open bullpen environments. I think it played a major part in avoiding disastrous appearances, and blowing the game for my team.. This played a major part in maintaining a consistently good ERA year after year. But, let's not overlook how important visualizing positive results and reinforcing them…really is.

As your self esteem rises…so will your ability to employ **the force**, and persist against all obstacles.

Fortunately, life doesn't have scouts or managers who decide who gets a chance to play. We all participate, and can find a way to surprise our friends, co-workers, parents….and ourselves.

This is the reason why you will be better than the competition…or your teammate….or other people with whom you must compete for a job.

It is a major weapon in your arsenal.

Having all of these things working for you…that very few people have, will feel really good. And, as your confidence and esteem rise…so will the assurance that **the force** will be there when you need it. After experiencing it… you can't help but feel more confident.

It is a wonderful self-feeding cycle…
and gets better and better.

I would like to amplify my example of
how important that element (of calm) is
with a one or two of my bull pen
stories:

As I said, I was a very nervous guy
and often sat in the bull pen, in the late
innings, when it might be my number
the manager was contemplating…
hoping we would get out of this jam.
Yes, that's right…**I was scared.**

But, if the phone rang, I was able to
control the fear, and concentrate on
what I needed to do. I found an inner
peace in "owning up" to my feelings.
Over the years, I discovered that
everybody has this fear…they just
hide it… or cover it up with macho
bravado.

In tight situations… when things became really "dicey"… I submerged the "scared" feeling, and was able to wrap an intense, but calm, **focus** around what I had to do.

OK, let's move ahead.

5. Accept responsibility…not just for your actions, but the actions of others.

As I said in the very beginning, as kids we are often protected to the point of expecting things to go just the way we want. When we get out on our own… with no parents or teachers to protect us, we are often lost and want to blame everyone or everything for our own failures.

I have often thought we would be a stronger nation…with better citizens…if every young person at age 18 or high school graduation (whichever came first) had a one year commitment to serve their country. It would start through military service…a form of "basic training". Everyone would learn how to follow orders, get in shape, learn a skill, and perform duties and "pay dues" for being born in the country of ultimate freedom. All would come away with a better feeling about ourselves, and with greater skills… to deal with what life brings. We all know lots of people who have an excuse for everything. That is not an option at "boot camp" .

This doesn't mean everyone would perform their obligation in the military. It could be as an aid in hospitals, filling clerical positions, Peace Corps, volunteer jobs, helping the handicapped, homeless etc..

What a huge asset in times of trouble. If a natural disaster or conflict (that threatened our nation) arose, we would have a trained force of twenty million "reserves" ready to step in and help immediately!

But, I digress. Back to your "future."

Taking responsibility for what you do (and what you failed to do) will shed the weight that has accumulated on your shoulders, and add another dose of that magic stuff… **Self-Esteem**.

6. Heed your Instincts:

Usually your initial "gut" reaction is the best. How often have you had the **feeling** you forgot something, but ignored it ? Chances are you paid the price… for leaving your putter on the counter, or your notebook at home, or "ouch" … remembering (you forgot) the keys to the cabin after a 200 mile drive.   Whenever you get that feeling, stop and analyze it.

Make a list. Check it again.

No wonder "an ounce of prevention is worth a pound of cure", is repeated so often.

Let's take this deeper than just forgetting something. Most of us are well aware of things we absolutely must do…plenty of time before it needs to be completed. Develop a plan and **get after it** right away…well before there isn't enough time to complete the task properly, and "heaven forbid", it is forgotten all together.

Here is what must be done: **Organize, schedule,** and **get started** on the problem, even if there's insufficient time to complete it now.

For over thirty years, I have used a three part system: 3X5 cards, a binder notebook (with my homemade calendar-day scheduler stapled inside), and my ever-present four color pen.

Why? In my case, it was out of necessity. I don't have a great memory, or attention span. Maybe a little attention deficit disorder might be a factor…not sure. But, you have magical "smart phones" and other digital devices. Learn how to work with their organizational tools…and **use them.** I'm working on it.

In spite of possessing an I Phone, the largest Outlook contact info list on the planet, and high tech patent filing software… I still like my four-color pen and the reality of my notebook…. with it's "see touch and feel".

It is comforting to know I can refer back to things, last week, last month or last year… and re-discover exactly what I was doing and thinking.

By carrying my "system" with me, and constantly referring to it (jotting down my plans for the day, with the critical ones in red) I have been able to avoid countless bad situations. There is a saying..."never enough time to do it right, but always enough time to do it over". It still may work in some developing countries…but with today's economic times, it is imperative that you get it right the first time. You can't afford to waste the time and money to start over.

Come to think of it… you now have most of my system. Grab that four-color pen and one of those 3 x 5 cards, and make a note….in red…to get a large note book to complete "the system."

Make sure you make it a double ringed binder. Otherwise, a year's worth of your life (or more) tends to come apart at the seams….

7. **Esteem**…is "**the word**" in this little book.

I have sprinkled building blocks to self -esteem throughout the book. Underlying everything you do, this one attribute is **essential.** Here are a few more tips…to help "fill your tank".

Being **helpful, kind and considerate to others** does more to provide instant gratification than just about anything else.

Every day is filled with opportunities. Open the post office door for the lady with packages, let someone make a right turn into your lane... pick up a piece of trash on your neighbors lawn... tell the waitress that you appreciated the great service... put a quarter in the meter just ahead of yours, as the meter maid approaches. Do this daily, and I can guarantee, you will be a new person. What if everybody read this and...did it? Worldwide?

It gives me "goose bumps" just thinking about it.

Try a little act of kindness on a person you dislike. You will be shocked and stimulated by how disarming and productive that can be....

I was in Saskatchewan Canada, duck hunting, many years ago. After a 4a.m. wakeup call and all-day hunting, I was "barely there" when I got a phone call from Judy at 9p.m..

She was distraught. She had just heard from the neighbor, who lived at the intersection of our two private roads. We were in the early stages of building a new home just down from that corner, and had gone to the trouble and expense of completing an extra-wide circular driveway, to make sure we didn't inconvenience our neighbors with any construction vehicles on the street.

This neighbor was screaming at Judy.

One of our construction vehicles had knocked a limb off their trees that hung over the private road. I "hung in there" long enough to call them and listen to part of their tirade. I promised to find out if anyone in our crew or subs was aware of this and make amends.

The next day, I talked to our general contractor…and he did indeed know what happened. It turns out that a utility truck was just ahead of him when he approached our job site. This EBMUD truck had nothing to do with our project and was headed to another location, when it hit the overhanging limb (an illegal invasion into the right of way). I had Joe clear the branches and explain to the neighbors.

No amount of factual explanation was going to convince them it was not our fault.

By the time we had moved in and gotten better acquainted with all of our other neighbors, it was apparent they were wonderful people.

Except the couple on the corner.

They had offended almost everyone in the area at one time or another.

A few years later the table were turned, and the couple (GG for short) were planning a major remodel of their own. But, they decide to block off their parking area by locking the gate, thereby, forcing all of the construction vehicles to park on the private streets, which were already narrow and really had no room to accommodate traffic.

This forced vehicles to squeeze by, often having to use our great circular drive to get past the "road block", just to get home.

During the construction, of course, the shoulder of the road across from their driveway was destroyed, mainly by the heavy loads of materials delivered to their job site.

GG had moved out due to the amount of work, and seemed it seemed they could care less about what they were putting the neighborhood through.

During our last 30 years or so in Lafayette (Northern California), we had accumulated a number of properties, and had also built several new homes (at various times) for our personal residence.

Every late fall or early winter, there would be a major rainstorm, which would cause lots of damage, as the debris, which accumulates during the dry summer and fall (from the leaves and various limbs and other obstructions), floats downstream to the culverts or drain openings. It invariably clogs the flow of surface water into the drainage systems, often causing minor to serious flooding.

So I learned to "plan ahead" and anticipate the events, and the prevention was priceless.

I was used to going on "damage control" during the first winter storm... with a pickup truckload of various tools and devices to solve the problems.

In the predawn hours, on the way out to visit our other properties...I noticed that a big load of lumber had been dumped in the street on the side of GG's construction site. The winds and rain had just begun, so I didn't see any problems...until I returned several hours later.

By then, the ditch on the far side of the road had become clogged, and flood waters were diverted to the other side...right where GG's newly delivered pile of lumber was dumped. I cleared the other side of blockages up and down Rancho View Rd, but the lumber was a pretty imposing diverter and directed all of the flood waters over the curb and into the middle of their downslope foundation.

No perimeter drainage had yet been installed, so it was only a matter of time before the whole foundation was undermined.

I worked for several hours and finally got the pile moved and the situation under control, and the storm drains back in shape to handle the flow.

Of course, there was no sign of GG. After all, it was early in the morning and there was a deluge out there.

I never told them what happened, nor that they probably would have suffered thousand's of dollars worth of damage as well as months of time lost. I assumed they would eventually get around to repairing the road in front of their home. After our construction, Judy and I had rebuilt the road completely in front, even though there was no damage. Seemed like the right thing to do.

When we moved from the Bay Area to Montana a couple of years ago, I couldn't help but notice (as we drove out for the last time) that the road was still untouched… and probably remains that way to this day.

Well…what's the moral ?

Who lost?…nobody.

Who gained?…me.

I put in a few hours of work, which probably was good for me. By my late 60's I could use a little exercise. All that wonderful conditioning from my baseball days had faded…but an occasional "reminder" was good for my body… and definitely good for the soul.

Sorry, for such a long story. But, it is one pretty special way to feel good about what you have done… in spite of your instincts.

From the storm drains, to a year in the Peace Corps, the bigger the deed …the more high-octane fuel goes in your self-esteem reserve.

Feeling good about yourself translates into a one word definition you will recognize…**confidence.**

Helpful, considerate, thoughtful behavior has another big benefit. **It is contagious!** However, none of those positive thoughts will help unless you **persevere** and avoid letting your ego overrule your respect for others.

8. Accommodate Failure.

No, I didn't say give in, or accept it. Just recognize that even the best efforts for the most noble objective… can come up short.

There is a common tendency to be afraid to take a chance. We have been taught that to fail is a disgrace. Nothing could be further from the truth!

Three strikes and…you're in!

If you haven't failed, probably you haven't really tried. **Not taking the risk for something you believe in, is the only true failure.**

So, forget your fear of failing and realize that if it didn't work…nobody died. The lessons learned will help you tweak your game plan, double your efforts, and quite possibly succeed the next time.

Even then, failure is a possibility. But, if you learn from your mistakes, get "bigger, stronger, faster, smarter" and still fail….**you are in a very special**

place.   You have built the most important ingredient anyone can have…and that is self-esteem. Rather than dejected, you will feel extraordinary.

When you dust yourself off a third time, you'll probably find that no one else had what it takes to try again. Chances are the opposition has melted away… and you **will have succeeded!**

That was the **single greatest lesson learned** in my career in professional baseball, and in my second occupation…real estate. Both demanded a high degree of personal belief, perseverance, and dedication.

It's a "one step at a time process", and the ability to learn from your mistakes and solve problems is vital, especially in baseball. At every level there were many examples of players with equal or greater talent. I succeeded (when many of these individuals did not) because I learned from failure, and redoubled my efforts at each crossroad.

9. Do it!

It is very tempting…not to put forth the effort that you know would separate you from the others…because it is often going to be tough, demanding, and time consuming.

When I began my career in the minor leagues, I started the first part of my "system"… 3x5 cards and a tiny notebook that fit in the back pocket of my uniform.

I kept a record of every player…what they liked and disliked, basically how they hit my "stuff." "Trades" explain why the loose "cards" in my back pocket were the weapon of choice. It was easy to change where they were filed, before adding to the notebook.

For me it was pretty repetitive. I was a "sinker baller". "Keep the ball down and get ahead with a first pitch strike" was the plan most of the time. But, occasionally I would learn something that defied the odds. Rod Carew was one of the best hitters in the game…in my era or any other. He wore me out!

Then I learned that a weak curve ball right down the middle was his "Achilles heel". Why? I suppose it was because he had great eyesight and reactions…and he was expecting a curve ball that actually broke!

My little spinner over the heart of the plate defied logic and gravity, but it frustrated the heck out of Rod. It worked… over and over again.

There was some good natured ribbing about all the work I put into those little books. But, invariably, the starting pitcher would pull me aside and want to "pick my pocket (book)" so to speak. I was happy to share…and know that my extra effort was vindicated.

I even kept a book on the umpires, their personalities and strike zone.   Umps remind me of traffic cops…they like the feeling of power and often had a bit of a chip on their shoulder. If you never showed them up (complaining or glaring after the call)… it was appreciated.

Hitters that "bitched and moaned"… often paid for it on the next call, or the following trip to the plate. It took a few years, but I eventually got more close calls than almost any other pitcher…because they respected **my respect,** for them.

We all need something to get us through the difficult times we have to face. It is not just you … everybody does. If you like having company… you've got it.

I met someone once who had a "flack jacket." This is better than a crutch, which is just something to lean on.

It went something like this:

Everyone needs three basic things:

Something to DO.
Someone (something) to LOve.
Something to HOpe for.

There's another acronym for you…**DOLOHO.**

Coming up with ideas… and daydreaming about success may be fun, but it doesn't get it done.

PLAN AHEAD, follow through, work hard… "keep the faith"(in yourself) and this little book close at hand.

May **DOLOHO,** and the **FORCE** be with you...

Use these pages for your "3 x 5" notes.

Made in the USA
Middletown, DE
24 November 2016